The Changing Face of
SALFORD

Cliff Hayes

A
Memories
Publication

ISBN 1 899181 25 3

Published by:
'Memories',
22, Crofts Bank Road,
Urmston,
Manchester.
M41 0TS
fax: 0161 861 7775

Layout & design by:
Acer Designs,
Manchester.
email: acerdesigns@aol.com
fax: 0161 881 8508

Printed and bound by:
Ashford Colour Press Ltd.,
Gosport,
Hampshire. PO13 0FW

Front cover photographs:
(top) Cross Lane, Salford in 1902, showing the Regent Theatre & Assembly Rooms and the Stowell Memorial Church.
(bottom) Ellor Street, Salford, in the 1960s.

Back cover photographs:
(from top to bottom)
The Imperial War Museum of the North;
An 'Eades' reversible tram waiting in Swinton before returning to Pendlebury;
Harold Hulton's Newsagents, on the corner of Duke Street & Clarence Street, Lower Broughton, c.1970;
The Lancashire Fusiliers Monument, Chapel Street, Salford, in memory of Salford lads who died during the Boer War;
Church Street, Eccles, before pedestrianisation in the late 1950s.

The Changing Face of
SALFORD

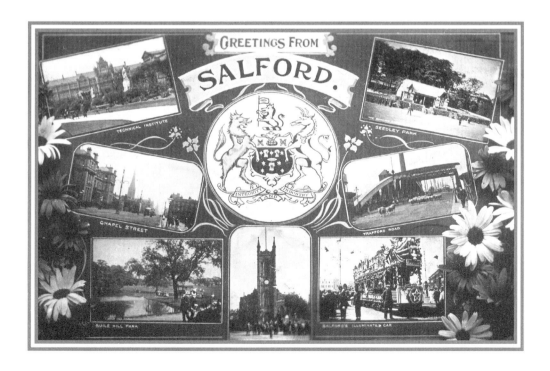

The original Charter, granted
to Salford by Ranulf, Earl of
Chester, c.1230.

CONTENTS

ACKNOWLEDGEMENTS

Thanks to Ted Grey for his help and guidance. To Tony Franklin, who is never afraid to point out any points of dispute in the books. To Tim, from the Local History Library, for all his help and to Tony Gibb for some of the unusual leaflets. Thanks must also go to Ken Craven who is part of the Lifetimes scheme which records the lives of Salford people. Billy Lines, next door, for some of the old street scenes, Ted Gerry for postcards. Thanks to Norman Connolly for the Leek St., party for the Queen's Coronation. Today's photographs come from the cameras of Vince Gillibrand, Ged McCann, and the author's own collection.

ABOUT THE AUTHOR

CLIFF HAYES was born in Ellesmere Port, Wirral and brought up in Widnes. He is 'A Lancashire Lad', regarding Widnes as Lancashire and Manchester and Salford as home. He has been associated with printing and the written word since he was eleven years old, when he had a part-time job scrubbing forms at a jobbing printers. Four years at the Liverpool School of Art taught him about design and printing and it also got him involved with the *Mersey Beat* magazine. He wrote for them, as well as providing a disc column for the *Weekly News* in the area. Jobs as a ships printer on round-the-world cruises and as a 'DJ' followed. Cliff has had a lot of experience, working in Blackpool, Liverpool and on the Isle of Man, before settling in Manchester and working on the *Daily Mirror* for 12 years. After leaving the *Mirror,* Cliff embarked on another new career, as publisher and author. His numerous books since then, for a variety of publishers, have done much to popularise the subject closest to his heart - the local history of the towns of Lancashire. Cliff's books reveal a vast knowledge and love of the people and places of the area. It is fitting that in his latest book, Cliff returns to Salford, the place to where the rover has returned and from where he started his publishing career. Cliff and his wife Sylvia live on the Eccles/Patricroft border.

HANKY PARK - THE PLACE AND ITS PEOPLE

'Hanky Park' was the name of an area of old Salford which still holds a special place in the memories of Salfordians worldwide. 'Hanky Park' is also the name that was adopted by Tony Downes and Peter Martin when this duo was formed, as a token of Pete's great love and affection for the city and its people.

Tony Downes began his musical career with Mike Harding. This partnership was to last six years until Mike's university life took precedence. Tony then became one half of the highly successful comedy duo, 'The Two Beggarmen' - a partnership that was to span some twenty years. When the 'Two Beggarmen' went their separate ways, Tony teamed up with Pete to form 'Hanky Park.

Pete Martin started his musical career in one of the many beat groups that thrived in the 1960s. Following a solo career, he teamed up with his brother to form a close harmony guitar/vocal duo called 'Me & Our Kid'. This act lasted fourteen years until his brother's circumstances changed, leaving Pete to revert to a solo career. Two years later he teamed up with Tony to form 'Hanky Park'. To date, they have four albums to their credit.

It is difficult to describe an evening with 'Hanky Park'. Their songs range from Lancashire folk to old-time singalong, with some songs from the 1960s. They also perform monologues and have a subtle, witty repartee. They provide all their own music with guitars and mandolin (no backing tracks or drum machines) but also work with backing musicians when the occasion demands. They also provide their own PA system.

Above: 'Hanky Park', a duo who capture the pride and spirit of Salford. Our photograph shows Pete Martin (left), Tony Downes (right). Contact Pete on 01706 221471 or Tony on 01706 840878

FOREWORD
by Pete Martin

"I remember how folks used to leave their front doors open and know their house was safe." "Only 'cos no-one 'ad owt to pinch!" I have lost count of the number of times I have heard that exchange of words.

Salford's own fire engines and police cars used to have bells (instead of deafening sirens) that could be heard from half-a-mile away. We used to watch and listen to the creaking of the crane at Cox & Danks from our bedroom - also half-a-mile away. Broad Street used to be so busy, with a wide variety of shops but there's not much left of it today.

I remember buying Noonan's delicious Ice Cream from a hand-cart and from a horse-drawn cart. We used to catch the train from Pendleton old station to Southport for day trips. The station has now gone, along with the canal that ran alongside.

The cotton mill next door, Elkhana's, burnt down and the lift now only travels between ground floor and basement levels. It now carries customers down to Copes Cash & Carry, instead of distributing bales of cotton to the three or four floors of the warehouse.

I started my working life as a shipping clerk, visited the docks every day - now that place has really changed! It used to be full of Lowry figures, now it's full of his paintings but, were they more at home in Peel Park?

Below and opposite page: The changing faces of 'Hanky Park'.
Right: The duo 'Me & Our Kid'.

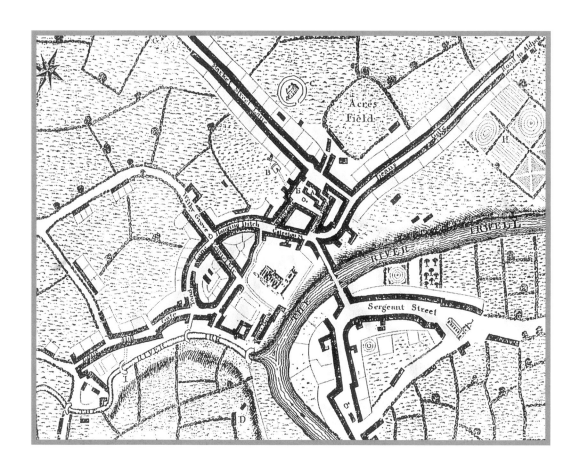

A MAP OF SALFORD'S MAIN STREETS AND THOSE OF ITS CLOSE
NEIGHBOUR, MANCHESTER, DRAWN AROUND 1650.

chapter one

AN INTRODUCTION TO SALFORD

SALFORD - The ancient capital of the Hundred of Salford and the Wapentake of the Court of Justice for the Salford Hundred set up by Edward the Confessor. The name Salford comes from Salixford, the ford where the willows grow. Salford, a market town in its own right: a township, a manor and a parliamentary borough. The Hundred of Salford precedes the Normans, though Salford and Manchester were governed by Commissioners.

In the Domesday Book Salford is mentioned as being the Capital of this 'Hundred', though sparsely populated and very rural in outlook. In the Anglo Saxon Chronicle, Salford features quite strongly and is noted as the property of King Edward the Confessor, (to confess in those days meant to tell everyone about The Good Book).

Let's go back about 1,000 years. Our area is mostly woodland and is owned by various Thanes and minor Kings. Twice the throne has taken the area back

Below: Broad Street, Pendleton, over a century ago.

under its control after unsuccessful uprisings. Roger de Poitou gave Manchester to one of his henchmen and the two cities were split for a thousand years, until Greater Manchester came along.

Rivers were clear, the Mersey was full of trout and salmon and it gave everyone a good living. The River Irwell by the Victoria station approach was thick with eels and eel pie was a Salford delicacy. The River Mersey was the boundary between Northumberland to the North and Mercia to the South and the River Irwell, after separating Salford from its near neighbour, ran into the Mersey, at Flixton.

Above: Ordsall Hall as it appeared in the 18th century.

In the early 14th century, when Lancashire was formed, Salford hung onto its name and position as head of the 'Hundred'. The Lord of the Manor held a power called 'The Liberty of the gallows, the pit, the pillory and the tumbrill' (treadmill) and could excuse a rich man anything, as long as he paid a hefty fine, whereas a poor man might well be hanged and his land sold off to another. Being Royal wasn't always to Salford's advantage. It was expected to contribute more to Royal collections such as weddings, births and raising armies. In 1168 Salford had to find £14 towards the wedding of Henry II's daughter.

The first recorded place of worship in old Salford was Ordsall Hall, which was constructed by the Radcliff family. Its first chaplain is noted in 1323. Trinity Chapel (The Flat Iron) was built in 1635. In 1650, there were moves to make Trinity into Salford Parish Church but nothing came of it. If Manchester was for Parliament, Salford was for the King.

When Manchester adopted Henry VIII's new Church of England, Salford stayed Roman Catholic, even though the faith had to be hidden. When the Nonconformists came along, it was Salford that gave a friendlier welcome to the Methodists, Congregationalists, New Connectionists, Unitarians and the most neglected of all, the Bible Christian Society, which did so much good and

Kersal Hall, also known as Kersal Cell, the home of the Byroms.

yet is almost forgotten. They published, from Salford, the world's first Vegetarian cookbook. They created Day and Sunday Schools, Soup Kitchens and so much more. The Recabites were also founded in Salford.

The Salford Court Leet governed the area from 1552 until 1886, when Manchester Assizes took over. Salford appointed, through its Commissioners, two Scavengers, a Catchpole, a Borough Reeve, a Tax-Gatherer and Night-Constables. Someone was once fined for 'eaves dropping' and standing too close when gentlemen talked. In 1600, another man was fined twelve pence for playing football in the street. All who came before the court were branded with an 'R' marking them as a ruffian. By 1800 Salford was a fairly well-run Borough, with gates closing the road into town and a set of rules to live by (no carrying of fire from house to house, for example). There was a Bread-Weigher and an Ale-Taster. Then waterpower hit Salford and mills started to spring up along the Irwell's banks. More people were needed to work at those looms and Industrial Salford had arrived. Engineering work took the town over. Mills and looms increased in number by the day and the population of Salford quickly doubled.

This is not a heavy book recording the exact history of Salford, but now that we have laid the foundation stones we continue, in photographs, to record . . .

THE CHANGING FACE OF SALFORD

Above: A very early drawing of the original Salford Cross, in Greengate, Salford.

STEPPING STONES IN SALFORD'S HISTORY

923	First reference to Salford in the Anglo-Saxon Chronicles, called it a village.
1086	Domesday Book stated that Salford was held by Edward the Confessor.
c1380	The Hundred of Salford was taken into Lancashire.
1399	The Duchy of Lancashire became a possession of Henry IV.
1070	William The Conqueror granted the Hundred of Salford to Roger de Poitou.
1142	Hermitage and Kersal given to Cluniac Priory of Lenton near Nottingham.
1199	Iorweth de Hulton gave Broughton and Kersal to King John in return for Pendleton.
1226	First mention of a bridge over River Irwell between Manchester and Salford.
1228	Salford received a Charter from Henry III granting a market and annual fair.
1230	The Earl of Chester created Salford a Free Borough and this Charter lasted until 1791.
1785	New Bailey Bridge across River Irwell opened. Became toll free in 1803.
1792	Manchester and Salford Police Act came into force.
1832	Salford became a Parliamentary borough.
1844	Broughton became a township and Salford received a Charter of Incorporation.

Above: Church of the Sacred Trinity, Salford.

1850	Public Libraries Act passed. (Salford already had a library, museum and art gallery).
1853	The townships of Pendleton and Broughton joined Salford.
1868	Salford gained two MPs.
1877	First horse-drawn tramcars started running in Salford.
1887	The Prince and Princess of Wales visited Salford.
1889	Salford became the first County Borough in the country.
1894	Ship Canal opened the world to Salford.
1896	Salford Royal Technical College (later University) opened.
1900	Twelve bridges over the River Irwell between Manchester and Salford.
1901	(20 November) Salford Electric Trams were formally started.
1908	Cussons family set up Soap Works in Kersal Cell Dyeworks.
1913	New H.Q. of Salford Temperance Society opened on the Crescent.
1915	The Salford Brigade was formed.
1919	Manchester Football Club (Rugby) opened at its present site in Moor Lane, Kersal.
1921	Salford Technical School took over from Royal Technical College.
1925	New market opened in Cross Lane.
1931	Salford Poor Children's Camp, Prestatyn, opened by Alfred Willett.
1954	Sir Malcolm Sargent became first president of Salford Choral Society.
1967	Castle Irwell racecourse purchased by Salford University.
1974	(10 June) Armorial bearings of Salford MBC approved and granted.

THE CHANGING FACE OF SALFORD

1978   Salford-born cancer charity worker, Pat Seed, received an MBE.

1979   Prince Charles opened the new Manchester Fire Brigade HQ at Pendlebury.

1980   River Irwell burst its banks, flooding homes in Kersal.

1981   De la Salle changed from grammar school to Sixth Form College.

1984   Huge Grain Elevator at Number Nine Dock was demolished.

1985   Salford City Council banned animal circuses from performing in the city.

1986   Built by local unemployed teenagers, the ship *Greater Manchester Challenge* was launched at Number Six Dock.

1990   Coal production ceased at Agecroft Colliery.

1994   Princess Anne visited Salford to mark centenary of opening of Ship Canal.

1999   The Metrolink Tram system began running to Salford Quays.

2000   The Queen officially opened The Lowry, on Salford Quays.

2001   Sir Rocco Forte's Lowry Hotel (five star) opened at Chapel Wharf.

Below: Early Salford depended a lot on the coal pits and here, from a hundred and twenty five years ago, is Clifton Colliery.

chapter two

THE STREETS OF SALFORD

Cross Lane, *below*, one of the oldest streets in Salford, as it looked just before the 1960s. Note the castellated Barracks building on the left hand side. This was the Territorial Army Barracks and was known locally as the Drill Hall.

There were two Barracks in Salford: the Infantry on Regent Road and the T.A. on Cross Lane. In 1968, Salford Corporation bought the Barracks and placed compulsory purchase orders on the pubs on both sides. The Barracks came down in 1974 to make way for the roundabout at the end of the M602.

The London North Western Hotel is the one showing the advertisement for Threlfall's Celebrated Salford Ale. Also in the picture is the Railway Hotel on the right and the Falcon, the white building on the left, which was just a beer house and not allowed to serve wines or spirits.

Cross Lane, Salford, taken from the corner of Eccles New Road c.1926. The Ship Hotel is just on the left and the Barracks can be seen further down Cross Lane. They used to say that there were so many pubs on Cross Lane that no-one could go down either side and have a half in every pub and reach the other end. This saying was also associated with other streets in Salford, in particular Regent Road.

Above: Cross Lane junction, looking down Trafford Road, with the Stowell Church on the right-hand side. Our picture shows clearly the complicated junction of tramlines that were once here. This junction was said to be the most complicated in Lancashire and has actually been lifted and stored at Crich Tram Museum, for eventual reassembly.

Above: Eccles New Road c.1920, as seen from Langworthy Road. Note the filling station for cars on the right-hand side. *Below:* Liverpool Street, c.1974. This street had shops from end to end before the M602 was built. Here we see Gallaghers Hardware Shop and Francis Ainsworth & Sons next door.

Lower Broughton Road from the Broughton Bridge end, in the mid-1960s. The dome on the right belongs to a public house called the 'Original' and at the left of our picture you can see 'Poets Corner'.

Cross Lane and Windsor Bridge c.1905. The centre of the pictures shows the cabmen's stand, where they would brew up and keep warm between fares. Behind that, to the left, is the Windsor Theatre, built in 1904 as the Hippodrome Theatre.

Above: The corner of Pendlebury Road and Bolton Road, c.1970. The second shop from the corner was a Chop Suey House, one of the first in Salford.

Above: The Flat Iron Market, next to Sacred Trinity Church. A busy market with hens, pigeons, rabbits and ferrets, as well as many second-hand bookstalls and cloth stalls. There are two explanations as to the origin of the name: the first being because the land was shaped like a flat-iron; the second because men from nearby engineering factories would use up bits of molten metal to make smoothing irons.

The Lodge at Ellesmere Park, c.1908.

Opposite page: Cross Lane and the corner of Liverpool Street, 1962. The first two shops, numbers 100 and 102, were Jones's Photographic and Chemist shop. People tell us that they used to hire a camera from the shop and, in the 1960s, it would cost you 2/6d per week to capture your holiday on camera. They also used to rent out a 'box brownie' camera for 6d per day including developing. This was handy for weddings and they used up the film taking family shots. Sometimes a whole street would club together and they would get dressed up and take everybody's photograph.

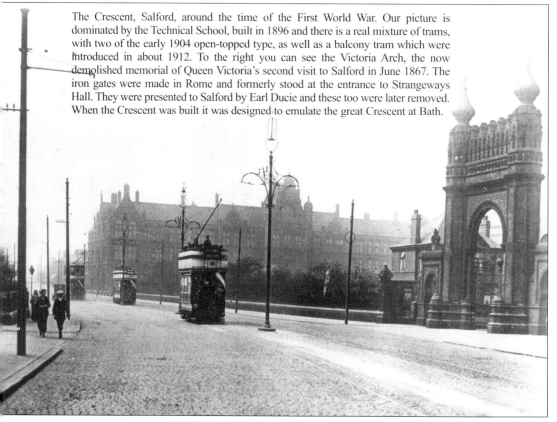

The Crescent, Salford, around the time of the First World War. Our picture is dominated by the Technical School, built in 1896 and there is a real mixture of trams, with two of the early 1904 open-topped type, as well as a balcony tram which were introduced in about 1912. To the right you can see the Victoria Arch, the now demolished memorial of Queen Victoria's second visit to Salford in June 1867. The iron gates were made in Rome and formerly stood at the entrance to Strangeways Hall. They were presented to Salford by Earl Ducie and these too were later removed. When the Crescent was built it was designed to emulate the great Crescent at Bath.

Left: Florin Street, on the corner of Coomassie Street, in the 1940s. Our picture shows the Coomassie Hotel, which actually took in lodgers and boarders. In 1873 Field Marshall Wolseley 'defeated the hordes of natives' in a West African uprising at Kumasi. Salford wanted to name a street in his honour but somewhere in the translation Kumasi became Coomassie. The mistake was pointed out but was never corrected. There are new houses on this site today, just by Salford Precinct.

A typical Salford street scene, in Florin Street, c.1960. Donkey-stoning the step was part of the daily ritual and you would be judged on how clean your steps were.

Above: Great Clowes Street and the Victoria Theatre, Lower Broughton, one of Salford's elegant Victorian theatres. Sir Henry Irving, the actor, laid the foundation stone and James N. Hardy Jnr., was the Manager when it opened on 10 December 1900. Our photograph comes from around 1920, when one of the delights of this theatre was its 'Jacobean Cafe' and its Afternoon Teas.

Above: Elleray Road, Irlam o' th' Heights c.1905. This was one of the private roads for the middle classes moving into the outskirts of Salford. Some of these private roads would have hired gatemen to check the comings and goings.

THE CHANGING FACE OF SALFORD

Left: The Horseshoe Hotel, in Broad Street, Salford, in the mid-1960s. The street once boasted no less than thirteen pubs, until road widening began in 1974.

Below: Ellor Street, on the corner of John Street, in 1960. The Advertising Standards of the day may not be being upheld, as the signs in the windows include 'The Cheapest Man on Earth' and 'The Working Man's Friend'. This is 1960 and yet there is still a woman wearing a shawl and a big pinny (apron) as she goes to the shops.

Above: Ellor Street in the 1960s. The road is still cobbled and the pavements are flagged. Far left of the picture, on the corner of Goodwin Street, is the UCLA Laundry. Customers had their own laundry book and number. Each week, they would note the articles handed in, ticking them off a week later, when they were returned. The laundry would be neatly folded, wrapped in brown paper and tied with string. These laundries were a step up from the wash houses. Next came the Laundrettes.

Above: The Blackfriars Street crossroads, looking down Chapel Street, c.1950. The Sacred Trinity Church is no longer used for services but is still a centre for church business. There are many memorial plaques and tablets on show here, from churches that have been demolished. Included in this memorabilia is the headstone of Humphrey Booth, who paid for this church to be built in 1635. He died on 23 July 1635 and was buried in the Cathedral across the river. His gravestone was found in 1894 and moved to the church porch, where bread shelves can still be seen. These were originally used every Sunday in the distribution of free loaves to the starving, paid for by the Booth charities.

Above: One of the roads that has changed completely is Cross Lane. Here we see it in the late 1950s, with shops from end to end.

Trafford Road, with Broadway to the left, the Clowes Hotel and the spire of the Stowell Memorial Church in the distance.

Below: Hankinson Street was the centre of Hanky Park. Our picture shows a 1930s view of the Lamb Inn.

A view of Broad Street taken in 1970. Broad Street was another of the all-shopping streets that was sacrificed to the almighty automobile. Boarded-up shops show work under progress into making the dual carriageway seven lanes wide.

Broad Street and the Pendleton Co-operative Industrial Society Limited.

A view of the famous Edmunds Stores, on Ellor Street, Salford - suppliers of everything from soft furnishings to 'Sunday best' suits. The store used to supply utility furniture during the War, for those unfortunate enough to have been bombed.

Hanky Park, looking towards Ellor Street and Tanners Lane. It is difficult to distinguish between bomb damage and slum clearance.

Above: The Empress Picture Palace and Ballroom, on Church Street, in the 1930s. This place started life as a skating rink and ballroom but, in 1911, the skating rink was converted into a picture house. The last film to be shown here was 'Greenwich Village', starring Don Ameche and Carmen Miranda, on Sunday 3 June 1945. For a few years it was the warehouse of a local firm that made crumpets. It was pulled down in the early 1960s, along with the rest of Hankey Park.

Above: The Palace, on Cross Lane, Salford c.1912. The Salford Palace and the Salford Assembly Rooms were actually in the same building. Animated films were shown there as early as November 1901 but the Palace had opened in September 1895 as a Musical Hall and was known as the Regent Opera House. It was built at a cost of £14,000 and seated 1,700.

Many a happy hour was spent in the local Corporation swimming baths. *Above* we see the Frederick Road Baths, which were demolished in 1970. They had opened in 1885, together with a wash-house and slipper baths. *Below:* Seedley Baths, on Derby Road. These baths were one of the last to be closed down, ending life in the early 1970s, after sixty years service.

A view of the large building on Cross Lane, Salford, which was the Regent Theatre and Assembly Rooms. The Regent went on to be called the Palace and our photograph shows the building in 1902. The Stowell Memorial Church can also be seen on the left of the picture.

Left: The Windsor Theatre, Cross Lane, opened as the Salford Hippodrome, in 1904. For a time it was a cinema but also such famous names as Frank Randle and W. C. Fields appeared there in live performances. In 1922, it changed to being a cinema and the first film to be shown was 'Why Girls Leave Home', a social drama. The Hippodrome was also used for amateur dramatics and was eventually pulled down in 1962.

Above: Broad Street, Salford, in 1970. Boots, UCP Tripe, Hardy & Co Furnishing and Dewhursts - all well known high street names - are caught on camera just a few months before their demolition, around 1971. The high rise flats began to dominate the area.

Above: Verandah shops, on Eccles New Road, c.1960. The shopkeepers used to look after their customers by pulling out the blinds on hot days and wet days, all as part of the service.

THE CHANGING FACE OF SALFORD

Left: The Craven Heifer public house, named because of the nearness of the Cattle Market. Our picture is probably from the 1950s. This hotel would take in guests including people waiting to join ships at Salford Docks. Many of the banana boats and African boats from Salford Docks carried up to thirty passengers on each journey.

Right: Salford Lads Club, built on land purchased from Salford Corporation when the old infantry barracks were demolished. The club was formally opened on 29 August 1903 and has kept records of every member who has since passed through it.

Left: The junction of Regent Road, Cross Lane and Trafford Road looking from Eccles New Road c.1930.

Right: Our picture shows the Trustees Savings Bank, Post Office and Midland Bank Limited, about 1965.

Left: Trafford Road c.1908. This picture shows three buildings that stood opposite the main dock gates - the Customs House, the Mission to Seamen (Flying Angel) and the Salisbury Hotel.

Right: The Langworthy Hotel, Seedley c.1920, when Langworthy Road contained a mixture of shops and private houses.

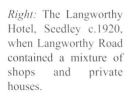

Victoria Bus Station at the end of the 1960s. Our view is looking from the station, down Chapel Street, into Salford. Because of the differences between Salford and Manchester Transport, Salford had its own bus station and interchange on the south side of Victoria Bridge.

Above: A close-up of the T.A. Barracks, on Cross Lane, Salford. The Seventh and Eighth Lancashire Fusiliers were in occupation in our Edwardian photograph. Note how ornate are the poles carrying the tram wire down the centre of the road.

Above: Trafford Road Swing Bridge in the 1930s. It was a feat of engineering that the electric tramlines could break and swing and then connect up together. Note the breakers on the front of the bridge. The bridge was swung using water hydraulics and the pump house, (now a pub) and water tower for this operation, can just be seen on the left of the picture.

Above: A 1966 view of Broad Street gradually increasing in width. Shops can still be seen on one side of the road, but they have not got long to go!

Above: The Woolpack, on Broadway - one of Salford's oldest and best known hostelries. This was the terminus for many of the Salford tram routes.

Above: Regent Road, showing The Fox Inn on the corner.

Above: The Bull's Head, a Groves & Whitnall's public house, reputed to be the oldest licensed inn in England. However, this did not stop it from being closed down in the early 1930s. After a fire in 1937 it was thought to be irreparable and was demolished at the end of that year. It was offered to Salford Corporation as a museum for a peppercorn selling price of £1 but the council did not take up the offer.

Above: The very poorest area in the centre of Salford was Greengate, seen here in a photograph taken by S. L. Coulthurst, in 1898. He would hide his camera in a suitcase and travel around Manchester and Salford taking true-life photographs, although this picture is obviously posed.

Right: This is a map of the wards and boundaries that received letters patent, raising it to the status of city, on 21 April 1926. This map comes from a 'Guide to Salford', c.1932.

Map of the Wards of the City of Salford

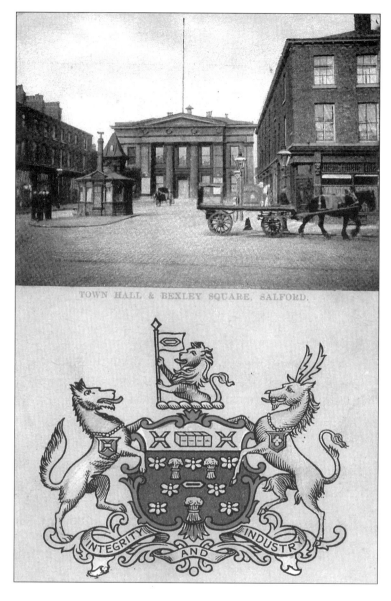

TOWN HALL & BEXLEY SQUARE, SALFORD.

Above: A postcard from 1926 showing Salford's Armorial bearings. The top half of the card shows Bexley Square, named by Lord Bexley, Lord Lieutenant of Lancashire. The impressive Town Hall overlooks the cobbled square that was to become the administrative centre of the city of Salford. Note the cabmen's hut, complete with stove pipe chimney. The bottom half of the card depicts the Arms of the County Borough and City of Salford. They contain three sheaves, which are connected with Ranulf de Blunderville, Earl of Chester, who made Salford a free borough in 1230. The crest on the top is a based on the Peel family crest and Robert Peel's connection with the area. The two supporters, the horse and the unicorn, are from the badges of the Duchy of Lancaster and the Earldom of Chester. The motto is self explanatory - Integrity and Industry. These arms were granted on 5 November 1844 and became obsolete on 31 March 1974, one hundred and thirty years later.

chapter three

1974 & THE GREAT SHAKE UP

When the Government decided, in the early 1970s, that new Metropolitan Borough Councils should be set up, local government boundaries were reorganised. The City of Salford gained Eccles, Worsley, Walkden etc., towns and UDCs that had always been on its fringe. What I found interesting was the battle over the new name. Among others, 'Irwellside' was suggested and even found backers on the council. Eccles was a very prosperous little town and did not want to disappear. They suggested 'Ecclesford', 'Salecclesly', 'Salden'. For a time it looked as if 'Irwell' would be the favourite but then common sense prevailed and the name Salford was chosen, leaving Eccles and the other areas as well-defined parts of this new MBC.

I remember, from a time when TV was in black and white, that there was a programme called 'What's My Line'. One edition had a lady (chip shop chipper) introduced from Eccles, Manchester and at this, Gilbert Harding protested that Eccles was a Lancashire town, just like Bury or Bolton. Consequently, the lady was re-introduced as coming from Eccles, Lancashire!

The new MBC found itself with many redundant Town Halls. Their fates have been varied: Pendleton pulled down, Eccles used for various youth projects and others boarded up. This chapter looks back at some of the areas which are now part of the City of Salford MBC.

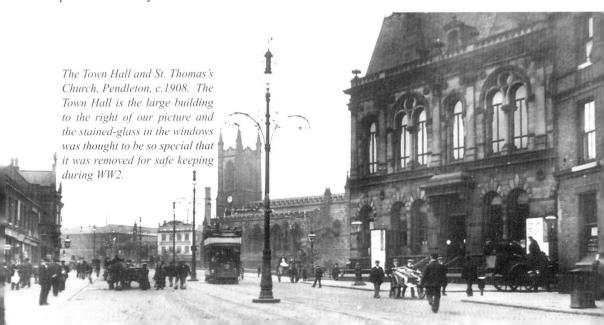

The Town Hall and St. Thomas's Church, Pendleton, c.1908. The Town Hall is the large building to the right of our picture and the stained-glass in the windows was thought to be so special that it was removed for safe keeping during WW2.

Above: The Bridgewater Canal at Monton c.1903. This is Brindley's Bend where plans were changed for taking the canal straight into Manchester and instead it ended up going over the River Irwell, round Trafford Park and on to Castlefield.

Above: Millbrow at Worsley from about 1920. Worsley was as far as the trams ran in that direction and the greenery and black and white buildings of Worsley show up well on this Francis Frith postcard.

Above: The end of the line at Peel Green and a tram waits at Liverpool Road tram terminus, ready to head back into Salford c.1910.

Above: The Co-operative Wholesale Society snapped up land alongside the canal, yet independent of the docks. Here we see their Soap Works at Irlam, on a postcard card from the 1920s. There was also a margarine factory and biscuit factory on this site.

Above: Eccles Railway Station, at the top of Church Street, was typical of the London and North Western Railway Stations that were built in the area. They all had one booking hall in the centre and the Ladies were usually to the right and the Gentlemens to the left.

Above: Some views change little over the years, while others change a lot. Here we see Gilda Brook Road, Eccles, in about 1959, looking down a very busy shopping street. The photographer was standing right outside the Railway station and you can just see the corner of it on the right-hand side.

Above: Looking down Church Street, Eccles, from the Railway Station, before pedestrianisation in the late 1950s. Service 64 with a Salford Daimler bus is coming up the street from the Cross at the bottom.

Above: Despite what you see in our picture and may have read in other books, this is the Ye Old Thatche shop, built in 1094, but it has nothing to do with the baking of, or making of, Eccles Cakes. It sold Eccles Cakes that had been bought from the original Eccles Cake maker.

Above: Eccles New Road, from Mode Wheel Road, Weaste, c.1930. This road has greatly changed, although the Grey Mare Inn, named during the days of coach and horses, is still there.

Above: A newly laid out Monton Green showing the freshly planted trees, c.1910. Note the open-topped tram heading towards Eccles. Salford trams never carried advertisements on their sides, just the name of the Transport Department.

Above: Broad Street, Pendleton, in a photograph from the very early years of the 20th century. St. Thomas' Church and Pendleton Town Hall are in the distance and on the right stand two of the four Non-Conformist chapels which were on this stretch of Broad Street. The Brunswick Methodist New Church, with its large steeple, is nearest to the camera. Beyond it is Pendleton Congregational Church.

Above: A busy Bolton Road, Pendlebury c.1910. The building with the large lamp outside is the Church Inn, opposite Christ Church. A typical working class area, with houses, pubs and shops all cheek by jowl, where people very rarely had to leave their locality. This picture of Bolton Road is taken from the corner of Chapel Street. I think that the chimney in the distance is Pendlebury Brick Works.

Above: Eccles Cross and Market Place, on a photograph taken from an Eccles Provident Industrial Co-operative Society booklet, dated 1907. Note that the horse trough, which stood in the centre of Eccles for many years, has supports which were designed to look like the legs of a horse.

Above: Scholes the Chemist on Church Street, Eccles. This building is one of the oldest in Eccles and still stands neglected today. Its daub-wall construction has rendered it impossible to use it as a chemist shop any longer because of the risk of burglary.

Above: A view of Eccles Cross, looking up Church Street, from about 1904. At the bottom right of the picture is the remains of the original Eccles Cross, which was taken away during the Second World War, after a lorry hit it during the blackouts. Nobody knows its whereabouts today.

Above: A wintery picture of Worsley and Worsley Court House. This photograph was taken just a year before the M60/62 motorway junction was to change the area forever.

The Packet House, Worsley, on the banks of the Duke of Bridgewater's Canal. Built about 1770 as three dwellings, which were then used as offices for the Bridgewater Canal and Packet Company. The black and white frountage was added in about 1850, when the Earl of Ellesmere wanted to beautify the village. The first passenger service from here was in 1769 to Barton and from the steps to Manchester in 1781. Today this is a Grade II listed building.

Swinton, picturing a horse-drawn tram waiting to return to Pendlebury. The tram is one of the 'Eades' reversible trams that turned on a central pivot, saving the need for the horses changing ends.

chapter four

TRANSPORTATION

Transportation, the matter of getting from A to B, has always seen Salford at the leading edge. The Bridgewater Canal was the first purpose-built canal in England. The canal system completely changed the face of the country and its way of distributing goods. The price of goods came down and materials began to move around more freely. Pottery, household goods, fresh produce and coal were all shipped by canal. The Duke of Bridgewater's Canal was the M1 of its day. It brought 'black gold', (coal), from Worsley, through Salford and beyond and heralded the Industrial Revolution. Salford was involved in the world's first purpose-built passenger railway, when the Manchester to Liverpool railway opened in 1830. It was to Eccles that MP William Huskisson was taken after his fatal accident at the Rainhill Trials.

Salford Corporation was at the front when it came to horse-drawn trams, electric trams and buses. Salford trams never had advertisements on the side. They did lend and borrow trams and buses in the Second World War. It brought smiles when they borrowed three buses from Wallasey and dockers on their way home were asked to 'shake the sand of their shoes before boarding' on a notice as they boarded the bus. Salford was the first to have strip lighting on buses and the world's first diesel engine lorry was converted in Eccles.

One of the most powerful steam engines to grace British Rail, LMS Coronation class 46257, City of Salford, seen here in 1950. This often did the Manchester to London journey without stopping, in time equal to today.
(photo courtesy Locofotos)

Above: The first electric trams were all open-topped and open to the weather for the driver. They did not have closed tops until about 1908. In Salford, the trams had pieces of tarpaulin on the stairs, known as 'modesty sheets', so that ladies going upstairs would not show an ankle. Here we see tramcar 24 on Eccles Old Road c.1904.

Above: A postcard of Salford's illuminated tram, decorated to celebrate 'Peace' in 1919 after the hostilities of the First World War.

Above: The scene at the junction of Eccles Old Road and Bolton Road, with the Woolpack just off the picture to the left. The traffic lights with their black and white markings date our photograph to c.1945. Trams were kept on during the Second World War because of petrol shortages.

Above: A South Lancashire Tramway Company vehicle entering the Salford area at Mosley Common, heading for Swinton in about 1904. You can tell this is not a Salford tram because of the advert on the side for Mellin's Food. Salford trams never carried advertisements.

Above: The tramcar 154 on route 71, at the junction of Cross Lane, with the Crescent (to the right) and Broad Street (to the left). Dominating the picture is Tommy Bradford's, the world-famous laundry equipment manufacturer.

Above: Oldfield Field Road, seen here in about 1930 from the junction with Regent Road. At its height, Salford had 75 miles of tram tracks.

Above: Salford's first bus just after its delivery in 1920. Note it is still an open topped vehicle complete with solid rubber tyres.

Above: Broughton Market Place, Higher Broughton, Salford, in August 1935. This part of Bury New Road was called Market Place but at the time of this photograph the market had long gone. The spire is of a church built by the North Manchester Society of the New Church, one of the many small Non-Conformist groups which settled in Salford.

Above: An open-topped tram, one of the two trams seen here inside Heaton Park. Heaton Park had its own branch line to take people right into the park to the boating lake. It was mostly used at weekends and bank holidays. Some of the line is still there and used by the Manchester Tram Preservation Society, which still runs trams inside the park.

Above: Local Radio Presenter Fred Fielder hosts a day out, including a look at the trams in Heaton Park.

Above: Monton Road, Monton, c.1910. Burgons Store can be seen on the corner of Highfield Drive, with the Circulating Library on the opposite corner. This was a stationery shop, which rented out books at 6d a time.

Above: Parrin Lane, Winton, c.1939. Shoppers pile on to the tram to go shopping in Manchester. Parrin Lane had a lot of single-track working, with numerous passing places.

Above: The bottom of Bolton Road, Walkden, picturing a Lancashire tram with a just visible index board stating Moses Gate. It looks as though this picture was taken during a special occasion. Perhaps it was the first through service from Salford to Farnworth and Bolton, which would date the picture to about 1908.

Above: Eccles Cross at the beginning of the last century. The photographer is looking up Church Street from the Cross and shows an open-topped tram travelling into Market Place. Although Eccles considered itself a separate town and borough from Salford, it did not have its own tramway and relied on Salford.

Above: A Salford Corporation tram heading for Deansgate, via Cross Lane. Note that even though the destination is shown on the side and front of the tram, numbers are also used.

Above: One of Salford's first buses seen coming down the Crescent, in May 1934.

Above: A view of the stone aqueduct at Barton, which carried the Bridgewater Canal across the River Irwell for more than one hundred years. The building in the distance is All Saints R.C. School.

Above: When the stone bridge at Barton became too much of an obstacle to the new Manchester Ship Canal, it was replaced by the famous 'swinging aqueduct'. The original canal is to the right and the aqueduct can be seen under construction to the left.

Above: A view of Barton Aqueduct, showing it swung to one side to let the ship *West Cressey* through, in the early 1920s.

Above: The Duke of Bridgewater left his estate to his nephew, Lord Ellesmere, who came North from London to oversee the workings of the Bridgewater Canal. He had a private barge built for him and his family and used it regularly. Here we see the barge on one of its pleasure trips, about a century ago.

Above: Greater Manchester Passenger Transport Authority existed before The Greater Manchester Metropolitan area. This brought all local buses under one management and adverts to the side of Salford buses. The photo is from September 1976.

Above: Eccles Bus Station, in July1954 and a 7' 6" Daimler bus waits to set out on Route 6 to Radcliffe.

Above: Salford bus number 288, (BRJ 942), leaving Eccles bus station with the number 54 service to Manchester, in July 1955. Salford buses were plain, clean-looking and offered a first class service.

Left: A Salford bus starts the 67 service from Brookhouse Estate down into Salford. The year is 1958 and the estate is still being built, as the background shows.

Right: A view from the cab of a bus as it approached Weaste Tram and Bus Depot, on Eccles Old Road. This depot had the largest unsupported roof in Britain, at the time of its opening.

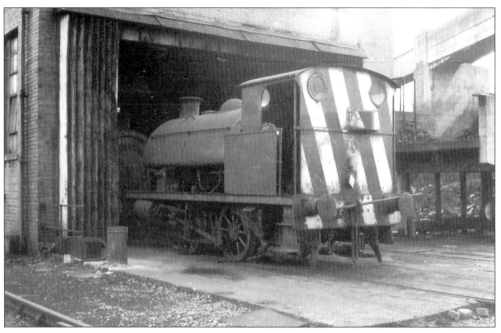

Above: Saddle-tank "Agecroft No. 3" was just used for shunting duties, in conjunction with Agecroft Power Station which had its own steam depot. The engine is seen here in February 1973, outside the C.E.G.B. shed.

Above: L.M.S. square saddle-tank no. 51230 waits in a line of shunting engines outside Agecroft Motive Power Depot. Trafford Park stored some of the shunting engines here, as well as goods engines for the collieries and power stations in south Lancashire.

Salford had another engine shed with larger passenger engines kept there. They supplied engines for the North Wales route and the Preston and Scottish lines. Here we see British Rail standard no.73130 passing Patricroft sheds, with an express bound for Chester, in March 1964. (Cooper's Railway photographs)

L.M.S. engine 44127 passes Patricroft with a freight train of mixed hoppers and ballast. Goods trains still had a guard's van at the back and steam brakes. Trainspotting youngsters nick-named these engines 'Coffee Pots'. (Cooper's Railway Photographs).

Above: 'Agecroft No. 2', just inside the engine shed at Agecroft C.E.G.B. on August 24th, 1975. The engine had just had a new boiler fitted and was waiting for a re-paint. (Locofotos)

Above: These little saddle-tanks did a lot of the donkey-work on industrial estates all over the North. They carried the water in a tank over the boiler, so it was half-boiled before it got into the boiler. For the record, it's L.M.S. engine no. 51207 inside the British Rail shed at Agecroft on June 21st, 1961.

chapter five

SALFORD DOCKS
AND THE MANCHESTER SHIP CANAL COMPANY

When the Manchester Ship Canal Company was looking for a suitable area in which to build docks, the only two places available were actually outside the Manchester boundary. The first choice was Trafford Park but Humphrey de Trafford would not sell to them. The second choice, at Ordsall, was sold to them by Lord Egerton and work commenced in about 1890 on building these docks, 35 miles from the sea. Salford Docks became the third largest port in England and, to keep the channel open, dredgers had to work constantly, keeping the depth just right for large sea-going ships. Even today, now that the shipping has gone, the canal cannot be abandoned because it is also the River Irwell and the water which runs between the two cities has to go somewhere. Turn your back on the River Irwell and Salford Quays would be under water and Warrington would flood.

It was a very brave decision to build docks 35 miles and a day's journey away from the sea. When it was first mooted, the promoters wanted it to be financed by ten shilling (50p) shares, to be bought by the ordinary working man. However, the money wasn't coming quickly enough and great men like John Rylands, Marshall Stevens, Lord Egerton, Platt and Mather, bailed out the venture. To compete with Liverpool, the docks at Salford had to work that bit harder and turn the ships around faster, in order to make up the day spent going up the canal.

Below: Mode Wheel Locks, the last obstacle to navigate on the Manchester Ship Canal.

Above: A view of the Mode Wheel Locks, from about 1904. The ship in the middle of the canal is one of the paddle tugs used by the Ship Canal Company to help the cargo boats dock.

Above: Number Eight Dock, about 1905 and timber from the Baltic is being unloaded on the far side. Salford Docks had to work hard to make profits and no dividend was paid out to the shareholders during its first eleven years.

Above: A busy Number Nine Dock, the last dock of all to be built. Elder Dempster, Manchester Liners, Clan Line and many others used this dock, which had been built on the land bought from the Manchester Race Company, which was formerly New Barns Horse Racing Track.

Above: The Manchester Fire Brigade, on Manchester Docks in 1900. The expected thousands of jobs for Salford men did not come immediately. The Ship Canal Company thought that the local workforce were untrained and so imported dockers from Preston and Newcastle. This caused ill feeling and it was not until after violent reaction from the locals that they agreed to employ one local man for every one 'imported'.

Above: The new footbridge between the Lowry Centre and the Imperial War Museum of the North had just been dropped into place when this picture was taken, in September 2000.

*Above left :*A grain hopper unloading the *Manchester Fame* which has brought its cargo from Canada. Most of the imported grain went on barges to the Kelloggs works, with one barge taking the load of fourteen lorries. *Above right:* The vast turning circle at the heart of Salford Docks seen here about 1937. As ships became more powerful they could dock, turn and head out with the help of tugs. This wide area of water is still there today.

Above: The *Princess Katherine*, the only boat to be seen regularly on the upper reaches of the canal today, rests alongside the newly finished Lowry Centre, in the year 2000.

Above left: A typical scene on Salford Docks unloading crates. *Above right:* A floating crane unloading the *Sibiu*. From Salford Docks there were regular and scheduled services to India, Indonesia, West Indies, Canada, New Zealand and even Japan.

Above: A cargo of frozen New Zealand lamb being unloaded from a refrigerated cargo boat in 1934. Note how much manpower was needed to handle this type of cargo.

Left: The floating steam crane at work about 1937. Over two thousand men worked at re-electrifying and re-coiling electric engines, stripping down and servicing diesel engines and the myriad of other odd jobs that went with the vast business of shipping.

Above: This is Number Nine Dock before it was completely flooded. In the centre of the picture is the grandstand of Manchester Racecourse. The steeple in the distance to the right is the Stowell Memorial Church. Manchester docks were numbered One to Nine but Number Five was never cut. It was marked out and left for many years before the plan was abandoned and the land built on. Docks One to Four are on Manchester and Stretford land, Number Five was never built and Number Six to Nine are in Salford.

Right: Dockers stand around waiting for the next crate to come out of the ships hold. Cotton bales are being unloaded here in the mid-1930s. When a ship is in port it takes on a whole new feel and the dockers and Customs officers are really in charge of the vessel, with the crew just waiting to get their ship back. Salford saw a lot of ships from the far east and there was a shop on Trafford Road that just sold sewing machines to these Goanese and Indonesian crews.

Above: A war-time picture of Salford Docks. The ship is painted in grey as camouflage and would have had guns mounted to protect it on its perilous journey across the Atlantic. These ships did a great job keeping Britain fed in the very dark years of the Second World War. This is Number Nine Dock and the floating grain elevators are unloading the precious cargo onto barges, ready to head for Trafford Park. (Photo courtesy of Manchester Ship Canal Company).

Left: Another ship leaves Number Eight Dock to head off on its next journey. I spent many years in the Merchant Navy and as that last rope drops away ships seem to shake themselves down and come to life again.

SALFORD DOCKS & THE SHIP CANAL

Right: One of the few lines that still use the Ship Canal is the Arklow Line. Here we see the bridge and ultra-modern controls of the *Arklow Trader.* This ship comes from Canada with grain for Cerestar, then picks up scrap metal and takes it to Spain. From Spain to Canada with wine and then back to Salford with more grain.

Below: The New Century Bridge, opened by Her Majesty the Queen in 1996. This bridge is another much needed crossing of the ship canal, to take the pressure off the Barton Swing Bridge further down. Here we see it in its raised position, ready to let one of the Arklow boats through.

Above: Another user of the Manchester Ship Canal during the Summer months is Mersey Ferries. They provide a cracking day out, taking sightseers up and down the canal. Here we see the *Mountwood* setting off in the Summer of 2001.

Above: A day out on the Manchester Ship Canal is a unique experience. The journey takes six hours and gives you an unusual insight into the area, seeing everything from a totally different angle.

Above: Barton Swing Aqueduct, after the bridge has swung away. A marvellous view of the barrier which keeps the water back. The aqueduct weighs twelve hundred tons and eight hundred tons of this is water.

Above: Barton Swing Bridge holding up the traffic as the *Arklow Trader* goes through. Being 'bridged' is part and parcel of living alongside the Ship Canal and this enforced hold-up gives you time to contemplate and slow down, as you watch the vessels glide by.

Above: Barton Road Bridge swung out of the way to let another ship pass. Fifty years ago there was an average of twelve boats a day going up and down the canal. Today there are not that many in a week. There is the odd ship going to the dry docks which still operate in Salford doing repairs.

Left: Salford Quays today. It may be a modern eating and shopping area but there are still many reminders around of its former uses. Two of the cranes have been moved to the head of Number Eight Dock, now called Ontario Basin, while Number Nine Dock is called after two of Canada's Great Lakes - Huron Basin and Erie Basin.

chapter six

PEOPLE AND PLACES

Salford has produced and nurtured some great characters and it has not been short of benefactors, philanthropists and charities. The earliest of these was the 'Booth' the Elder charity, founded in 1630 and still going strong today. Other charities include Humphrey Booth's (the grandson of the Elder), founded in 1695; Dickannson's charity (1711), Broster's (1787) and Armitage's (1887). There are other charities still going today which still help Salford's poor.

I used to think that it was the drinking water from the River Irwell which gave Salford so many characters but the Irwell has not been used for drinking since industry arrived in Georgian times. It must be in the air in the close, tightly-knit streets and terraced housing. Life was tough in Salford in the early 20th century but people got by. They made their own fun and entertainment with good humour. There were 'Diddle-Ums' (Savings Clubs), Christmas Clubs, Pub days out, Sally Army Suppers etc., all forming part of the Salford scene. I often think that Salfordians and Liverpudlians have the same sense of humour and determination to make the best of life.

Amongst the many celebrities associated with Salford are Jimmy Jewel, Will Hay, Al Read, Ben Kingsley, Robert Powell, Alistair Cook, Harold Riley, Albert Finney, Ewan McColl, and L.S. Lowry. All these and many more were born in, or spent much of their lives in, Salford. *Below:* Regulars, barstaff and family members gather outside the Horse & Jockey, on High Street.

Above: The 'Flat Iron' market Salford, in the early 1900s, with Abe Sachs selling one of his famous £1 suits. He would throw in a pair of braces to make it more of a bargain.

Above: The Flat Iron Market, Salford in the 1920s.

Above: Shoppers hunting for bargains at Salford Market in 1961.

Above: A very sad-looking Ellor Street in the early 1960s, with its empty shop premises, prior to the redevelopment ot the area.

Above: A typical teenager showing off his new motor cycle. Whenever the camera man turned up, kids would gather to be in on the picture. This one was taken c.1930.

Left: The Whit Walks in the 1960s. The procession heads down Regent Road, which would have been closed to traffic, while churchgoers, Sunday School children, brownies and cubs proudly took part.

Above: All clean and tidy 'angels and cherubs' pose for their school photograph, in 1954, at St. Sebastian's, Gerald Road, Salford. *Below:* The Queen's Coronation in 1953 was celebrated with street parties all over the country.

Above: Black's shop, Broughton Lane, well stocked and ready to serve their customers

Above: Mr. Frank Jones and his son, Norman, outside their wallpaper store on Whit Lane, about 1953. They advertised free trimming, a chore that needed a steady hand and a sharp pair of scissors. The half inch of white paper along either side of the patterned paper was where the printing machine roller had gripped it and it had to be cut off each roll. The Elephant and Castle pub is on the left and Armistead's confectionery shop is on the right.

Above: The Wash House on Hodge Lane, in 1930. Salford was one of the first to introduce an all-electric wash-house and would boast that 'washing day has turned into a day of happy work. In cheerful company, the housewife can finish her family wash in two hours'. Unfortunately they had problems with the electrical machinery and it was never fully operational. *Below:* Children from Halton Bank Primary School pose for their photograph, in 1938. (Photograph courtesy of B. Harrison, front row extreme right).

Above: A postcard commemorating the Queen's Golden Jubilee in 2002, produced by the Wise Monkey Theatre Company, depicting episodes in the long history of Salford.

Left: Broad Street Restaurant, one of the four 'British Restaurants' opened in about 1940 in Salford. They were opened with Government money to make sure that working men got a hot meal and people who had lost their homes were fed. At the British Restaurant on Trafford Road they started with two hundred sets of cutlery, within a week there were less than one hundred. The manageress started charging 2/6d for the cutlery refundable as you left the restaurant. By the end of the month there were over three hundred sets of cutlery!

Above: Alderman Sydney Hamburger officially opening the new Fire Station in Broughton, on 23 June 1964.

Right: The interior of St. Thomas's Church, Pendleton, as it appeared at Christmas 1926. It was built in 1831 and seated 1,200 people. Today it is a landmark, towering over the roundabout and what is left of Broad Street.

Above: Dignitaries waiting to greet King George V and Queen Mary during their visit to Salford on 14 July 1913. Salford was once a thriving industrial town and had many Royal visits, in acknowledgement of its importance in creating wealth for the country.

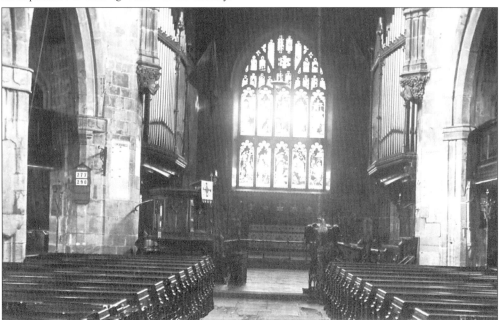

Above: The interior of Eccles Parish Church (St. Mary's) from about 1931. When it was first built, in 1525, it had the title 'The Ancient Church of Our Lady of Eccles'. The church has many interesting features and artefacts, including part of an ancient Celtic Cross and the Brereton family tomb.

Above: Salford's Mayor, Edward Arthur Hardy, greeting King George V and Queen Mary when they visited Salford on 17 July 1934.

Above: A personal Christmas Card from a Worsley family, Christmas 1949.

Above & left: Laurence Stephen Lowry, born in Stretford in 1887, was an enigma in life. He moved to Salford (Pendlebury) in 1909 and stayed there until 1948. Lowry moved again to a house called 'The Elms' at Mottram-in-Longsdale where he spent the rest of his life, until his death on February 23rd 1976. He is buried in Southern Cemetery with his mother and father and others of his family, with his name in small letters on the side of the cross that marks the grave.

He was a simple man who cared little for the high and mighty. He would chat to the children before dropping a few pennies on the ground and move on. Once, when a man from the *Times* newspaper knocked on his front door to interview him, Lowry pretended to be his imaginary brother Fred and told the reporter that LS the painter chap had gone on his holidays. The reporter had to return to London without his interview.

He once said: 'Heaven alone knows why I came to this awful place. I hate the house I live in now' and as the years wore on he would spend more time either with friends or in hotels on the East Coast, an area he had come to like. He enjoyed his record collection (mostly classical) and he loved the radio, a favourite programme being 'Housewives Choice', listening to it in the front room. He didn't bother with television. On meeting him, he seemed awkward and slightly ungainly but there was something about him that made most people refer to him as 'Mr. Lowry'.

PEOPLE AND PLACES

Right: The Essoldo, Ford Lane, Pendleton c.1959. Tucked away behind Pendleton Church, it was originally built as the Scala but, like many other cinemas, it took the name Essoldo after being taken over by a Salford Company. I am told that the Essoldo Company was owned by a man named Solomon, his wife was Essme and he had a daughter called Doreen and 'Essoldo' comes from these three names.

Below: Going on days out with the school, or Sunday school, was a real treat. Here we see the choir boys from St. Sebastian's Church, Pendleton, on a day out to Burtonwood, in 1952.

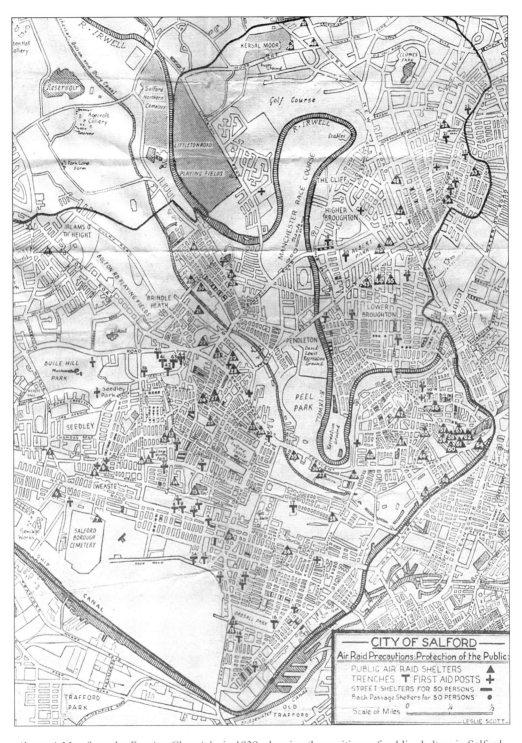

Above: A Map from the *Evening Chronicle*, in 1939, showing the positions of public shelters in Salford.

Above: Salford was one of the first Rugby League towns and at most schools was the first choice of youngsters over soccer or Rugby Union. Here we see Clarendon Secondary School Rugby Team, in 1960.

Above: The Park Hotel, Monton, in the late 1950s.

About a hundred years ago, an African Prince came to live in Salford. He was Peter Leslie Lobengula, who had been driven out of Rhodesia while fighting for his father, King Lobengula, against Cecil Rhodes' forces. In England, he starred in a show called 'Savage South Africa'. It was very popular and made a lot of money for the theatre manager, who promptly disappeared (wages and all). A dejected Lobengula languished in Salford until an usherette, Lily, took pity on him and they moved in together, living in Phillip Street, Pendleton. He got himself a job as a coal miner down Pendleton Pit and they moved to Gladstone Street, off Indigo Street, Pendleton. They had son, Peter, who was in the Salvation Army and a daughter called Victoria. He had a lot of trouble getting on the Electoral Register and had to go to court to get his vote in West Salford.

After he contracted Tuberculosis, he applied for a Rhodesian pension but was rejected. Prince Peter Lobengula died of Tuberculosis, aged 38, on 24 November 1913 and was laid to rest in a pauper's grave in Agecroft Cemetery. Lily Lobengula died on 27 February 1920 aged 39 years.

Some cast doubt on this story but I believe it. Someone else must have believed it also and they put up the cross. *Above:* The gravestone of Lily Lobengula and *left* is the cross to commemorate the life of Peter Leslie Lobengula.

98

Above: Trafford Road, Salford on an Edwardian photograph. You can see the Salisbury Hotel in the centre of the picture and the Custom House on the right. You can just about make out the dock wall on the left of the picture.

Above: Trafford Road in 1990, taken from outside the Dock Gates, looking towards the swing bridge. You can see Starvin' Marvins, which was the first American-style diner in Britain, imported from the USA to stand on Trafford Road. Unfortunately it was burnt out after about eighteen months.

There used to be a local saying 'Salford goes to Manchester for its education, but Manchester comes to Salford for its entertainment'. The pubs in Salford were just that bit livelier. The Music Halls were noisier and the jewel in the crown was the racecourse at Castle Irwell. The family who owned Castle Irwell did not like the races being held on their land. The racecourse moved for a few years (1886-1901) to New Barnes, which was an area at the side of the docks. The first Manchester November Handicap was held

there but New Barnes was eventually sold to the Ship Canal Company and it became Number Nine Dock. Today, as you drive away from the Lowry Centre towards Eccles, you are following the last furlong and run-in at the New Barnes racecourse. The finishing post was where the tram station is today. *Above:* The New Barnes racecourse at Salford Docks, in about 1900, at Whitsuntide. The Whit meeting was always a crowd-puller and one of the busiest at the course.

Left: Bookie, Alf Bailey, dressed as either a Chief Engineer or Chief Steward, taking bets at Manchester Racecourse in the 1920s.

Above: An aerial view of Manchester Racecourse, in 1965. It had closed down after the November Handicap in 1963 and sold to Salford Council for University accommodation. This desolate view shows the River Irwell curling around the old racecourse site, with Kersal flats and Agecroft power station and colliery in the distance. (Photo Miss N Barrett). *Below Left:* Manchester Racecourse c.1960. *Below Right:* The advertisement shows the number of racing days that there were each year.

MANCHESTER RACES

WINTER and **SUMMER RACING**
under ideal conditions

The **RACECOURSE "DE LUXE"**

SEVEN MEETINGS	SEVENTEEN DAYS ANNUALLY
NEW YEAR	Victory Steeplechase
FEBRUARY	Grand Allies Steeplechase
MARCH	Minden Rose Steeplechase
EASTER	Lancashire Steeplechase
WHITSUNTIDE	Manchester Cup
SEPTEMBER	Prince Edward Handicap
NOVEMBER	Manchester November Handicap

The Racecourse can be reached
BY AIR   Barton Airport, Manchester (12 min.)
BY RAIL   All Manchester Stations
BY ROAD   Direct to Motor Parks Entrances

Admissions
2 6 Ring (Uncovered Stands)   New 6 - Ring (Covered Stands)
Grand Stand and Paddock   Gentlemen 21 -   Ladies 10 -
LARGE MOTOR PARKS

TOTALISATORS IN ALL ENCLOSURES

ROBERT L. BUSBY, Secretary,
The Racecourse, Manchester, 6

Above: The popular radio show presenter Wilfred Pickles and his wife Mabel arriving at a Charity Show for Children, given at Hope Hospital in about 1950.

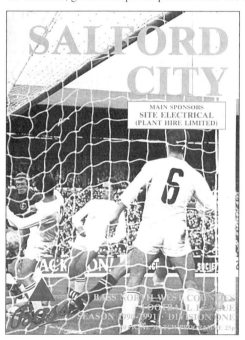

SALFORD GREYHOUND TRACK
(OPPOSITE MANCHESTER RACECOURSE)

Equipped on the most
up-to-date lines.

A FINE TRACK AND
GREAT SPORT.

NEW HANDICAP RACES

COVERED STANDS IN
EVERY RING.

REFRESHMENTS.   CAR PARK.

TUESDAY, THURSDAY,
FRIDAY and SATURDAY
EVENINGS at 7-30 p.m.
THROUGHOUT THE SEASON.

PRICES: 3/6   1/6   1/2
(TAX INCLUDED)

Under National Greyhound Racing Club Rules.

Ladies admitted free by official
Race Card at all Meetings to end
of Season.

SALFORD
GREYHOUND TRACK
OPPOSITE MANCHESTER RACECOURSE

Salford has a long sporting history with its own soccer and rugby teams, the horse racing and the greyhound track. Many a day at the races was rounded off by an evening at the greyhounds, *above right,* which was just across the road. Salford Rugby League Team were known as 'The Reds' long before that other team took over and *above left* we see a programme of Salford City when they played in the Bass North West Counties League Season 1990-1991 Division One.

In 1930, Salford celebrated the 700th Anniversary of its Charter with a magnificent Historical Pageant, held in Buile Hill Park. Important events in Salford's long history were re-enacted by players in the park and the next two pages show Pageant scenes taken from the Pageant Programme that was produced at the time. *Above:* The Pageant Programme cover is shown.

PROLOGUE. *The Rose of Lancaster and Attendants*

PROLOGUE. *Father Time and The Spirit of Salford, with Attendants*

(By kind permission of the "Daily Express")

Glimpses from the Episodes

Salford Choral Society formed in 1948, just after the Second World War. It is a very important part of the cultural scene of Salford. *Above:* Here is a c.1950 photograph of a concert that was held in the Great Hall of the Technical School, with Frank Rushton conducting. *Below:* Norman Beckett conducting carols in Lark Hill Place, in Salford Museum & Art Gallery, in the 1950s.

Above: The Salford Choral Society practicing for their first Concert in the new Lowry Centre, where on 2 December 2000 they performed the 'Messiah'.

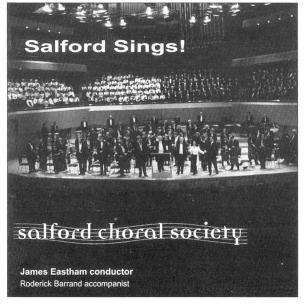

Right: 'Salford Sings' is a CD of the Salford Choral Society and a great listen. It was released in December 1999 to celebrate the Society's 50th anniversary and also the Millennium. Salford Choral Society is a registered charity and you can contact their Publicity Officer, Mrs C. A. Saltmarsh, on 01942 795086 or by email at: salfordchoral@ntlworld.com

Left: St Philip's Church, St Philip's Place, Salford is a Waterloo Church, built in 1825 by Sir Robert Smirke. It was almost an exact copy of the church he had just finished in Wyndham Place, London (St. Mary's). It has had a very chequered history but still stands today as it was a century ago. Here we see the church from Chapel Street with its tall tower and domed top.

Below: Here we see St. Philip's church from the organ console. The church seats 1,700 people, 700 on the ground floor and 1,000 in the balconies. The Salford Choral Society rehearse here on Wednesday nights and the Northern Chamber Orchestra play here with a regular programme of music. The church has been used for many classical and light music recordings, as the acoustics are excellent.

Above: The organ of St. Philip's Church, Salford, exactly as it was installed. Because this church is a Waterloo Church and Queen Elizabeth II acknowledges the title Lord of the Manor of Salford, it has the Royal Coat of Arms displayed on the balcony. The tower and its clock is now maintained by Salford Council.

Right: Looking back down the aisle from the altar of St. Philip's Church, the Royal Coat of Arms and the organ can be seen. In the film 'Hobson's Choice', Maggie married Will Mossop in this lovely church and it was on this spot that the camera filmed John Mills waiting nervously for Brenda de Banzi to turn up.

Left: The Roman Catholic Cathedral of St. John the Evangelist, photographed in the year 2000, from Chapel Street. Building began in 1845 by Weightman & C. Hadfield of Sheffield and was finished around 1848, although not topped-off and consecrated until 1855. Salford Roman Catholic Diocese was formed in 1850, with an enlightened view that Roman Catholics should be allowed to build their own places of worship.

Below: Our photograph shows the East Window, which depicts the history of the Catholic church in Lancashire. This is a very busy and vibrant church, which includes a Bookshop and Visitor's Centre.

Above: Here we see Bishop Sharples at rest in Salford Cathedral. The brass plaque on the floor is to Bishop Holland and the other plaques are to all the former Archbishops of Salford

Right: The inside of St. John's Cathedral, in about 1900, before it was modernised and stripped of all ornamentation.

Above: A picture of the Memorial to the Leeming family, who donated most of the money for the building of this lovely Cathedral. They are buried in a crypt under the great West Window (not beneath this Memorial, as you would think). The Leeming family were very forward thinking and were amongst the first to sponsor flying from Hough End and later Barton, which helped in the formation of the Manchester Aviation Club.

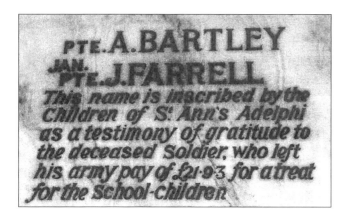

Left: Inside Salford Cathedral is a Memorial to the men from the area who died in the Great War. Under the name of Private J. Farrell is an inscription denoting that this young soldier left his army pay for a treat for the local school children.

Above: St. Paul's Church of England Church, Paddington, Salford, is a church with a very chequered history. It was built around 1845 by the Church Commissioners and was the last Waterloo Church to be built in the area. It cost £4,856 and was designed by Shellard; the parish was small at 70 acres but with a population 7,500. All around it has changed but the church remains more or less the same and it has even taken on another parish.

Right: We see how the landscape around the church has changed, with the terraced houses having been replaced by tall flats.

Lawrence Gardner was born in 1840 and described himself as an machinist. After he died, in 1890, his three sons, Thomas, Edward and Lawrence, bought three acres of land from the Leigh family and began building their Barton Hall Engine Works. The Barton family originally held the land and built a hall there before it was passed to the Booth family of Eccles. Through marriage the land then passed to the Leighs, who sold it off. *Above:* The Barton Hall Engine Works as it looked in 1908 and *below* we see men and apprentices at work in the factory in the same year.

Right: An aerial view of Gardner's works in 1968 taken to celebrate the company's centenary. The photograph shows how large the machine shops were. Roughly five thousand men worked there in the 1920s but today most of it has gone and what is left is used as individual units, with only a few used for engineering. The success of Gardners engineering was that they made engines that did a specific job. They made engines for dentists' chairs and road rollers; they converted the first lorry from petrol to diesel and they did it with their own designs, not by following Dr Diesel's German patent. During the war years, they made tanks and armoured vehicles but they were probably best known for their partnership with Rushton, in making diesel shunting engines for British Rail and other railways world-wide.

Below: The machine shop at Barton Hall works, in 1908. *Above:* A late 1960s photograph of the main engine shop in Barton Hall Works. Eccles and Salford were famous for their engineering works. James Nasmyth and his steam hammer, Sir James Farmer Norton and many others had large works in Salford. Where have all the engineers gone?

Above: An early 1990s photograph of the Farmer Norton works being demolished. The works stood at the back of Salford Royal and had been there for over a hundred years. They specialised in making machines for wire-drawing.

The Acme Mill being demolished in the early 1980s. The chimney of the FEB works standing nearby was also demolished at the same time. (Photo: F. Wright)

chapter seven

SALFORD TODAY

People on the outside of Salford see it as a problem area but in fact Salford has no more problems than any other city or MBC. It has its upper and middle class areas, with a scattering of large mansions, including historic buildings such as Ordsall Hall, Kersal Cell and Monks Hall and it also has its problem areas. Salford Quays has been a great success, breathing new life into the old dock area, creating not only living space but a venue for music and the arts.

Where is the centre of Salford? The old centre is now an abandoned area used as a car park. The old Town Hall is still used as a Court but some of the shops and public houses around it are boarded up. The Civic Administration comes from the Civic Centre at Swinton, *pictured below*, nearly seven miles from the original centre at Greengate. In times gone by people would say that a market marked the centre of a town or city and while this was true of the Flat Iron Market, held near the Sacred Trinity Church, it was not true when Salford Precinct opened. The Precinct and Market was a deliberate effort to create a shopping and socialising area to cater for all classes of Salfordians. The market was moved from Cross Lane after fifty years, into a modern centre with Public Houses, a Meat Market and Post Office standing along side Marks & Spencer,

the Fifty-Pence and a Pound shop next to the Co-op and Holland & Barrett. This shopping precinct has had very mixed fortunes over the years and, at the moment, it seems to be on a low with the loss of some of the better shops. Last year there was a chance to build a new City Hall and Administration block, where Trinity Way meets Chapel Street. This could have taken in the old Gas HQ and the other buildings recently renovated in the area and Salford would once again have been run from its old centre. Flats are now going up on that land and everyone connected with the Council seems to be content to run Salford from Swinton. That leaves the new retail complex, next to the Lowry Centre on Salford Quays, where parking can be costly. A shopping development at Eccles (West One) seems to be very much out of people's way.

Salford has many sides to the image it shows the world. It is too often shown on television in a negative way but, as someone who lives in the area, I have tried to capture all of its aspects, both good and bad in this. . . .

CHANGING FACE OF SALFORD

Above: During the construction of the Lowry, seen here in 1999, an ex-docker phoned Allan Beswick on local BBC Radio and asked if they had found the UXB that had landed at the entrance to No. 9 dock in 1941. This stopped work for about a week but metal detectors couldn't find the bomb. To nit-pick just a little, if you visit the Lowry you have to brave the weather from the car park to the theatre and the concrete dust everywhere, on your big night out. The promised Metro line to the Lowry was never built, through lack of funding, even though the points and branch-offs are there ready. Theatre parking is quite expensive and this has to be added to the cost of the ticket. It is still a lovely place for a peaceful cup of coffee and it does attract visitors from all over the North West.

Right & below: These two pictures show the Lowry Centre rising from the old entrance of No. 9 dock. The Lowry and the adjacent retail outlets were built at a cost of £127m. The Millennium fund put up £64,000,000, Salford and private investment found the other half. Once the project was announced for the Millennium it was always certain to be

completed, unlike many other projects which fell by the wayside. The Lowry centre opened on time in 2000 and it is a great success. Both photographs were taken in 1999, from the deck of HMS *Bronnington*. It was a shame to lose the ship from Salford Quays but parking charges for the Imperial War Museum of the North made it too expensive for most people to visit the ship.

Right: This looks like a spotlight in front of the Lowry Centre and here we see it just after it had been dropped into place, in 1998. How many people know that the world's first Lime Light was demonstrated to the public at Buile Hill, Salford?

Above: The Imperial War Museum of the North, though it is in Trafford, dominates much of Salford Quays. The building represents the world shattered into four pieces and spread out on the ground. Our photograph shows HMS *Bronnington* moored next to the museum. I still think that the ship would have been a great addition to the museum's features and am sorry to see it go to Birkenhead.

Above: This picture shows just how vast an area of water is at Salford Quays. The Commonwealth Games Triathlon was held here with great success. Our photograph is taken from the restaurant and bar area of the Samuel Platts on Trafford Wharf Road.

Above: HMS *Bronnington* was a great loss to the Salford Quays area. The parking area, which for many years was free when you visited the ship, suddenly became the property of the War Museum and charges of £3 and £5 were introduced. What is the point of the Government making museums free to visit when private companies run their car parks at outrageous prices? I really thought the *Bronnington* had a part to play in the story of warfare. It was built of wood so that magnetic mines would not be attracted to it and this is the only preserved example. The ship had Prince Charles, The Prince of Wales, as its Commander for four years and we are led to believe that he did some of his courting of Princess Diana aboard the ship. *Below:* In 2002 the *Bronnington* left for the War Ships collection in Birkenhead. Here we see a lovely shot from the bridge, just before she left, featuring the Morse signalling light.

The Metro tram has arrived in Salford. The Princess Royal, Princess Anne, officially opened the line. It only really skirts the south of the city, going through Salford Quays and on to Eccles. *Above:* The line being built to go over the roadway on Salford Quays. There was a lot of construction work and a lot of disruption in the area, but now the line is working it all seems worth it.

Left: Here we see another view of the construction work at Salford Quays Station. The line is running and passenger numbers have exceeded expectations but what has happened to the spur line into the Lowry Centre?

Above: Here the construction work crosses the turn-off to the Customs & Excise Offices and on to Salford Anchorage station. Trams have to be supported on special running rails, due to the weight of each double-vehicle, which is six times that of the old street trams, which ran on railway lines sunken into Salford's cobbles. Who chose the tram's names? They could have been so much more local and appropriate.

Right: The tram arrives at Eccles, the end of the line. So much more could have been done! The public, the Trafford Centre and all concerned are waiting for the news that they can take the tram into the new Trafford Centre. Extending the line would cut down road congestion and bring more business to the Centre, with Manchester at the other end of the line. However, the powers that be do not seem to want to push ahead, even though the track is laid right to the Trafford Centre.

Times changed and falling class numbers meant that many schools became redundant in the 1980s and 90s. Here we see two views of Ordsall High School during demolition. Sadly, nothing had been built on this site five years later. One of the teachers at Ordsall High, overlooking the Docks, was local historian Ted Gray and he tells a great story about a Dock crane driver with a bike. Apparently this crane operator used to lift his bike up into his high cab with him. There were no clocks on classroom walls and kids didn't have watches but every day, at lunchtime, this bike would swing past the window as the driver went home for his dinner and the kids knew that this was the end of morning lessons.

Above: Water has always been an attraction to youngsters of all ages. Our subject is not walking on water but was caught on camera shortly after having jumped off Ontario Bridge, during the school holidays of 2002.

Right: Salford Quays attracts many colourful visitors. The 'Walk the Plank' ship and its entertainment has been here for many years. Here we see the *Golden Hind* replica on a visit to the Quays, in 2000.

Above: Some parts of the old docks haven't changed in the century they have been here. The gates of the Manchester Ship Canal Company remain the same, even though all around them has changed.

Left: Around the Lowry Centre building work still goes on. Here we see apartments going up in 2002 and development still continues to the present day.

Above: The old Number Nine dock in the Spring of 1990, looking very picturesque. It's reminiscent of 'Legoland' with its pointed roofs and identical new buildings.

Right: At Salford Quays there are plenty of reminders that this was once a thriving dock. The cranes, the tying-up bollards, all serve to keep the memories alive.

Above: Langworthy Road, Salford, runs from the start of the East Lancashire Road right down to the former Salford Docks. It was named after Edward Ryley Langworthy, who did so much for Salford (along with his brother). Our picture shows the middle section of Langworthy Road, once a mass of shops from end-to-end. That's the Langworthy Hotel on the right of the photograph.

Above: Langworthy Road is undergoing a facelift and here we see some of the shops being pulled down. The Langworthy Cinema was a silent-movie cinema and Violet Carson (Coronation Street's Ena Sharples) was once a pianist there. It was turned into a convenience store and has now disappeared altogether.

Above: Langworthy Road in about 1938, featuring the Langworthy Hotel on the right. It was, at the time, quite a high-class establishment and the function room upstairs was the place for 21st birthday celebrations, wedding receptions and other social events. For some reason, funeral receptions were always staged down stairs in the Commercial Room.

Above: A very rare postcard of the inside of the Langworthy Hotel, in 1904. The potted palm and drapes, the Commercial Room and the Snug (ladies didn't go into the bar). Our postcard says it all.

Above: Here's a reminder of how the docks looked when they were in their prime.

Above: The Mersey Ferry *Mountwood* leaves Salford Quays for a day trip down the Ship Canal. These trips are very popular and attract large numbers of people.

Right: Buile Hill is a mansion that should be one of Salford's jewels. It was built between 1825-27, for the Potter family, to a design by Sir Charles Barry, one of the leading architects of the time. When William Potter became Mayor of Manchester he continued to reside here in Salford. The top storey was added later by local architect, Edward Walters. Our photograph shows the House in its prime, pictured on a 1904 postcard. It was sold by Mrs Mary Bennett to Salford

Corporation for £23,000, including 80 acres of ground for a public park. Arc lights & electricity were first demonstrated here on 7 August 1850 and, as it was the home of the Mayor of Manchester, many meetings and balls were held here. I wonder what happened to all the fixtures and fittings from here?

Left: Buile Hill is a lovely park for leg-stretching and dog-walking. The greenhouses here were used to grow all the plants for Salford's civic buildings and functions. The outhouses have become a Social Centre and are well-used. Here we see Buile Hill today, with 'Keep Out' signs and railings round it. Salford acquired it around 1902 and it opened as a Natural History Museum on 30 May 1906. I went there a few times later when it had become the Lancashire Mining Museum. I thought this was a great museum, especially for youngsters. Upstairs was a bit boring, with types of helmets and Davy Lamps etc., on display but the ground floor had a 'pit cage' which took its passengers down to a basement 'coal mine'. It was only about fifteen feet down but you did get the feeling of being underground, stepping over mining equipment to get to the 'coal-face'. It was very well done and a great shame that it closed. There were a lot of coal mines around Salford but it seems that the city is not proud of the fact and does not care about handing the memory down to today's youth.

Above: Down comes Salford Royal Hospital! In 1827 the Duchy of Lancaster gave land at the end of Oldfield Road for the building of the Royal Salford & Pendleton Dispensary. In 1860 it changed from a Dispensary to a Hospital when ten beds were added and the building enlarged. By 1870 there were thirty beds and four wards, opened with the help of Thomas Pendlebury's £30,000 bequest. It was a 'recommending' charity and only someone who subscribed to it, or was 'recommended', could be a patient.

Above: Here we see work to turn the shell of the former Salford Royal into luxury private flats. Our photograph was taken in 2002.

Above: Salford Royal Hospital in 2002 showing the massive redevelopment. It was from here that a mass radiography unit - the first in Britain- was brought into use in 1945. Salford was also the first smokeless city in Great Britain.

Right: The front of Salford Royal Hospital on Chapel Street, showing the portico entrance and Royal Crest, given by Prince Albert who donated money to the hospital's charity.

Pictured above is the White Horse, on Gilda Brook Road, Eccles, in 2003. If this pub were nearer to the Salford Racecourse I would automatically assume that the horse in question was Snowball. Snowball was quite a character. He was a big cart-horse, employed to pull the rollers and other grass-cutting equipment along the river bank, skirting the racecourse.One day, while harnessed to a heavy roller, he accidentally slid into the river. A great cry of 'save Snowball' went up and the racecourse staff rushed to help the beleaguered horse, trying to unharness him and keep his head above water. The fire brigade and a vet were sent for, as everyone struggled to save the horse from drowning. Suddenly, the mid-day hooter went and lo-and-behold, Snowball pricked up his ears, struggled and, with a bit of effort, walked out of the water unaided. He went up the bank and straight to the stables where his dinner was waiting. This caused much hilarity and the story is still told today to everyone's amusement. I would like to think that this pub is named after dear old Snowball.

Above: One building with an uncertain future is the Manchester & Salford Bath Company building on Collier Street, Greengate, Salford. It was a Public Baths for over a century and then used as a match factory .

Above: A rare photograph of the inside of the baths. It really is too important a building to demolish but what is Salford going to do with it?

Above: The Sacred Trinity Church as it is today. Much collecting of religious interest material is done from here and they have published quite a few leaflets on other religions in the area. Many memorials from disused former churches are stored here.

Left: Salford Corporation's Model Lodging House, built around 1890 to house the itinerant workers in the area. Our photo is from 2002, as it was being turned into flats (like everything else in the area). Salford's Coat of Arms can be seen above the arched entrance to the building, where lodgings were 2d per night when it opened.

136

Above: Here we see the Royal Coat of Arms above the Court House in Encombe Square, Salford. On it is the motto 'Dieu Et Mon Droit' (God And My Right).

Right: The gateway to Salford Courthouse. Many have passed through here on their way to prison, including England's one-time most wanted murderer, Charlie Peace, who shot and killed a policeman in Chorlton.

This is the latest bridge to link Salford to Manchester, designed by Dr Santiago Calatrava. The red-brick building in the distance is the old Threlfalls Brewery on Bloom Street, off Chapel Street.

Above: The Church Inn, Liverpool Road, Eccles, c.1995. A very historic inn and the building where John Moores, founder of Littlewoods Pools and Liverpool's John Moores University, was born in 1896. Many local history societies fought for a Blue Plaque to be put on the building, without success (see below).

Above: The Church Inn was sold to the gas company behind it and before you could say "Bless You", it had gone - demolished without trace. All this for more storage space for gas, which many consider is too close to schools and housing.

Above: The Packet House at Worsley. Built by the Third Duke of Bridgewater, it was originally three dwellings, one of which sold tickets for the journey to Manchester. The black and white timbers of the building were added on the instruction of the Earl of Ellesmere.

Left: A close-up of the black and white building which has become so famous over the years. The round plaque on the side of the building commemorates the Bridgewater Canal as Great Britain's first purpose-built canal.

Above: The steps at Worsley where passengers would board the packet boats. Queen Victoria once disembarked here. During the 1980s the steps were left abandoned and became overgrown. They have recently been cleaned up and are now an interesting historical feature of the area.

Above: Spring 2003, looking towards the start of the Bridgewater Canal. We must remember that a major purpose in the construction of the canal was the drainage of the mines at Worsley and that it is iron deposits inside the coal mine which give the water its reddish colour. It was a wonderful idea of James Brindley's c.1750 when he made the suggestion: 'Let's not pump the mine, let's run it off.' The canal is unique and this system of drainage was a hundred years ahead of its time.

The photographs on this page show the dereliction of the oldest Catholic Cemetery in Britain. The land on Peel Green Road, Barton, was given by the de Trafford family in the 1820s, when Parliament passed the Roman Catholic Emancipation Act. Salford Local History Library has a list of all the families who are buried here. Salford have been threatening to buy the land since 1975 but so far things have been left to deteriorate. *(see below)*

City of Salford
City Technical Services Department

City Technical Services Officer
and Deputy Chief Executive
William C. Roberts, B.Sc., C.Eng., M.I.C.E.,
A.R.I.C.S., M.I.Mun.E.,
M.Inst.H.E.

Town Hall, Salford, M3 6DH
Tel. 061-834 2363   Telex 667671

My ref: V/TAT/RM/6290
Your ref:
Date: 2nd December, 1975
Subject: DISUSED BURIAL GROUND ADJOINING
            NO. 12 PEEL GREEN ROAD, BARTON, ECCLES.

Dear Sirs,

The Corporation has recently purchased land to the rear of the above burial ground and plans are in hand for its development for housing. It is hoped that access may be provided from land adjoining No. 24 Peel Green Road.

At a recent site investigation attention was drawn to the derelict condition of the burial ground . I am, therefore, wondering whether you would consider a sale to the Corporation in order that the site may be incorporated within the housing layout. The object would be to use the land for landscaping/amenity purposes only with all building and accessways restricted to land already in the Council's ownership.

My Valuer has had a preliminary word with Father Dalston of the Holy Cross Church and understands that he can see no objection to this suggestion.

Yours faithfully,

William C. Roberts

City Technical Services Officer.

Above: The United Reform Church, Chapel Street, was built in 1819 of brick, with five arched windows. It is seen here in 2000. *Below:* The Mission Hall on the corner of Broadway and Trafford Road. This huge building is used by many people including Ordsall Citizen's Advice Bureau.

Above: A timeless picture of the River Irwell flowing by the Crescent in Salford. It could have been taken any time in the last 50 years but was actually taken in 2000 while recording a Radio 4 programme to go out in celebration of the Lowry opening. It was here that they shot the final scenes for 'Hobson's Choice', adding loads of detergent to the water in order to produce 'authentic' foam on the river whilst filming.

Above: It's been there for over 230 years and is part of the life of Salford. This photograph shows the Bridgewater Canal as it heads for Barton Aqueduct.

Above: The airport at Barton is now used for small light aircraft and microlights. At one time this was Manchester's official airport, with booking offices on Deansgate and coaches taking passengers out to Barton for their flight. It was not the first 'Air Receiving Station' in the area - that was at Trafford Park, then at Hough End during the First World War.

Above: Gardner's Engineering may have faded from the scene but the works are still there as our photo from Easter 2003 shows.

Above: No, this is not Stratford-on-Avon, it's Barton-on-Irwell. There's the monastery and the Swing Bridges and, nearby, flocks of swans and Canada geese that have made this their home. The swans make a lovely sight down at Barton and 2003 was a good year for cygnets.

Above: The swing bridge on Trafford Road doesn't swing any more and is now just one-way, carrying traffic from Trafford Park into Salford Quays. It's a shame that it lost its historic wickerwork signal-baskets (look on the older pictures and you will see them there on the bridge). Salford's Trafford Park workers would watch for the baskets going up to warn of an approaching vessel. They would then jump off the bus and run across the bridge so that they were not late for work and lose 15 minutes wages.

Above: This is the gravestone/monument to Marshall Stevens, the man who steered the ship canal through Parliament. He also developed Trafford Park and made it a success. He was MP for Eccles and a great believer in votes for all, including women. He and his sons ran Trafford Park Estates for a hundred years. He was one of the world's greatest experts on transport and organisation. He even organised his own funeral and this 20 ton slab of Cornish granite was mined from near his place of birth.

Right: Marshall Stevens, the man who never got the recognition he deserved. He really should have had at a knighthood. His hobby was writing gardening books and gardening was his way of relaxing.

Above: A drawing of Ordsall Hall from about 1850. The first house was built on this site c.1251, by David de Hulton and in 1360 Sir John Radcliffe built a hall here for a branch of his family. In 1639, the west wing was rebuilt in brick, by Sir Alexander Radcliffe.

Above: Here we see a postcard of the kitchen, just after it opened as a museum in 1972. The Hall came into the Egerton family by marriage in 1758 and stayed in the family until it was bought very cheaply by Salford Corporation in 1959, from the trustees of the Tatton Estate. The Hall would have been lost if Wilbraham, Earl Egerton of Tatton, Viscount Salford, had not decided to restore the building and turn it into a clergy training school. It had been used as a working men's club by Haworth's Mill.

Above: The back of Ordsall Hall and part of the original house. In times past, the Hall was much bigger than we see today and was moated. The part we call the back of the hall today was once the front.

Above: Ordsall Hall seen here as it was in 1990, before the glasshouse was added on to this nearside. How they got away with adding a glass conservatory (now used just for storing chairs) to a 15th century building I will never know. They did, however.

Salford Shopping centre just five years ago, with W. H. Smiths and Marks and Spencer as two of its main attractions. Both have now gone, with M. & S. having moved into the Trafford Centre, despite saying they were not going there. We see Mays on the right of our photo, *above*, Salford's oldest pawnbroker. They are an institution and have been in business in Salford for nearly a century. *Below*, we see Albany Way as it is today, with the former Marks' still not occupied. John Menzies became W. H. Smith and is now a £1 Bargain Centre. This spot was formerly the end of Ellor Street and part of the old Hanky Park.

Above: Eccles as it is today and here we see the end of Church Street. Church Street turns the corner at the cross and goes down to the library, with its memorial to Laura Davis outside it.

Right: The Eccles Cross as it stands today, in a sorry state. I really think it would be nice to find the original cross, which was taken away in 1939 for wartime safe-keeping. The stained glass windows of Pendleton Town Hall and Salford Cathedral were put away at the same time and returned. So where is the Cross?

Above: The Royal Technical College, the Crescent, Salford, was opened in 1896 as a three-storey, red terracotta building by Henry Lord. Since becoming a University many buildings have been added to this original centre. Now, I have got to get this of my chest: *Eastenders* came up here some time ago and did two weeks of filming, with Bianca supposedly going to Manchester University. Actually, all the filming was done here but they didn't want to call it Salford! That's southerners for you.

Above: Lark Hill Place is a fascinating place to visit and what great memories it evokes! It's free and it's open on a Sunday. Everyone should make a point of visiting the Living Museum there in the Library and Art Gallery. Our photograph shows the chemist shop window, with its Indian Brandy, Caster Oil, Syrup of Figs and salt pillar. Oh, the memories!

Above: The Shoe Makers shop in Lark Hill Place. One-up, one-down houses have been preserved here with stairs that were just ladders screwed to the wall. It really is an interesting place to take the youngsters. Make a note of it.

Above: Here we see the outside of the Art Gallery and Museum. Before the Lowry opened, this building held the greatest collection of Lowry paintings in Britain. I once bumped into Mr. Lowry in here and chatted for a few minutes. The building started life as Lark Hill, the home of Colonel Ackers. William Garnett lived there later, before he moved off to the Lake District, donating the house to the people of Salford. North and South wings were added in 1852 and 1857. The building as we see it today was completed in 1936-8. The Local History Museum is in this building (see back page).

Above: One of the new features around Salford is this cast-iron Sycamore seed, placed between St. Philip's Church and Salford Cathedral. It was made by local apprentices and is an attractive addition to the area.

Above: Regent Square, Salford, as it is today, just a quiet residential street.

Above: Salford has some lovely old buildings but they are not appreciated as much as they should be. Here we see the old Town Hall which started life as a market hall on the ground floor, with local administration done from the first floor. The building took two years to complete and was started in 1825. It was opened by Lord Bexley (Lord Lieutenant of Lancashire) and the square was named after him. Richard Lane was the architect and it is in the Greek Doric style. Today it is the Juvenile Court for Salford.

Right: These were the Gas Board Offices in Bloom Street and it is a very impressive building, complete with a balcony for speeches. There was once a gas scandal in Salford, with the works manager getting a kickback when he sold off the coke but that's too involved to go into here.

Above: Monk's Hall, Eccles, seen here from the front. It was owned by the Council for many years and was a museum before it was sold. It became a French Restaurant when Grant Chapman bought the building in 1997. It is one of the oldest buildings in the area, with the back of the building still as it was in 1600. It was called Monk's Hall Grove and rebuilt, in c.1840, in the style that we see today.

Left: Here we see what I believe is the Victorian electricity supply unit, looking very ornate, at the back of Monk's Hall in 2003.

Above: An old view of Kersal Cell, Salford. It was the alleged birthplace of John Byrom who wrote the hymn 'Christians, awake'. Whether he was born here, or in the Wellington Inn, is still a matter of debate but the Cell was one of the Byrom family homes. It started life as the cell for monks of the Lenton Priory, a Cluniac House. Elizabethan wall-paintings and a 17th century staircase remain here. Kersal Cell was scheduled for demolition but was saved by a Salford Councillor who bought the property and opened it as a night club and restaurant.

Right: We see the building today as two residential houses. How nice it must be to live with so much history around you. John Byrom was a real character who learnt to sit on the fence in the torrid years of witch-hunts and anti-Catholicism. He survived Bonnie Prince Charlie's visit to Salford, as well as Charles II's 'purification'. He invented the first shorthand so that Catholics and Protestants could write to each other. When ordered by Prince Charlie to address the Cathedral on St. Andrew's Day, Byrom came out with these famous equivocal words:

God Bless the King, our throne defender,
No harm in blessing the Pretender
But who is Pretender and who is King
God bless us all, that's quite another thing.

Swinton Shopping Centre, Lancastrian Hall and Central Library. This redevelopment took place after nearly twenty years of talks. Two hundred and seventeen houses, fifty shops, three offices, four small factories, three clubs and a betting office were all demolished to make way for this new shopping centre. *Above:* We see the Lancastrian Hall and Central Library as it is today. *Below:* One of the shopping centre entrances with such shops as Clinton Cards, Boots the Chemist - all the usual retail outlets.

Above: The entrance to Swinton Market. The centre was opened on 16 May 1969, when Ken Dodd did the honours. On 6 March 1970, the Lancastrian Hall & Central Library were opened by the Rt. Hon. Jenny Lee, the Minister for the Arts. Designed by Leach, Rhodes & Walker, it has a fully equipped 32 feet by 24 feet stage complete with revolving centre.

Right: The sun sets on the Lancashire Fusiliers monument, Chapel Street, Salford. On 13 July 1905 the King came to Salford to unveil the statue, which was erected to commemorate those Salford lads who died during the Boer War.

LIFETIMES

Lifetimes is the name of an exciting visitor attraction at Salford Museum and Art Gallery, phase one of which opened in May 2002. Lifetimes brings the history of Salford to life by revisiting both everyday experiences and major events, from Royal visits and Whit Walks, to wash-days and schooldays. It charts the history of the whole of the city, from Walkden to Winton and from Pendlebury to Pendleton - as seen through the eyes of Salford's people, old and young.

Visit Lifetimes at:
Salford Museum & Art Gallery,
The Crescent,
Salford,
M5 4WX

email: info@lifetimes.org.uk
tel/fax: 0161 736 1594
Open: Mon-Fri, 10.00am-4.45pm and Sat/Sun 1.00-5.00pm. Admission FREE

SALFORD LOCAL HISTORY LIBRARY

Salford Local History Library is a great FREE resource available to everyone.

The library's extensive collection includes:
Family History Sources,
Maps,
Newspapers from 1858 to present day,
Photographs - more than 50,000 local pictures,
Local information.

The library's friendly staff are always happy to help you. Visit the Salford Local History Library at:
Peel Park,
The Crescent,
Salford,
M5 4WU

tel: 0161 736 2649